North American
Wild Animals

By Colleayn O. Mastin *Illustrated by Jan Sovak*

Grasshopper
BOOKS PUBLISHING

Beaver

Beavers are their busiest
When their forest world is dark;
They're skilled at cutting trees down;
Their favorite food is bark.

Beavers live in families,
And none can sit and dream
While the others "work like beavers"
To dam a pond or stream.

Beavers are wonderful builders. They build their lodges of sticks and mud. These homes are called dams because they trap the water supply beavers need. Beavers can stay under water for a long time because their extra large lungs can store great amounts of oxygen.

To build their dams beavers use small trees and branches, which they get by gnawing through tree trunks until they fall. The beavers then drag, float or carry the branches and twigs to their homes. The lodge is ruled by the female.

Not all beavers have to build dams. Some dig dens in the mud in the banks of rivers and deep lakes all across North America, except for the Arctic tundra, Florida and the desert areas of the Southwest.

Beavers are busy animals, gnawing and cutting trees to store away as food for the winter.

Beavers have strong teeth that keep growing all the time. They also have broad, flat tails covered with scales. If danger is near, they slap their tails on the water to warn other beavers of danger. Their enemies are the wolf, fox, coyote, wolverine and man.

Beavers mate for life. Their babies are called kits. The kits stay with their parents for two years, when they are sent off to start their own homes and families.

The beaver is the national emblem of Canada and is North America's largest rodent.

Black Bear

Bears are very small at birth,
But they grow up heavy and tall;
Their fur is rough and very thick,
Their eyes and ears are small.

Bears aren't fussy eaters—
They eat both meat and plants;
They're especially fond of berries
And salmon and honey and ants.

Black bears live in the forests and woodlands of Canada and the eastern and central United States. Their fur is brown, cinnamon, white or black.

The den of a bear may be under a tree stump or in a hole on a hillside or any other sheltered cozy spot. Female bears usually line their dens with grass, ferns or leaves so they are comfortable and cozy for the cubs. Males usually do not make their dens so comfortable.

The female bear is called a sow. She is about three years old when she has her first babies. During her long winter sleep, one or two cubs are born. It is hard to believe that these creatures that grow so big are only the size of a rat when they are born.

After the cubs are born the mother bear stays away from adult males because they have been known to kill the young cubs. Mother bears protect their cubs fiercely and stay with them through their second winter. In the spring of their second year the youngsters are left on their own and the sow mates once again.

Bears sleep through the winter, but they do not truly hibernate. Their body temperature does not fall, but their breathing slows down a little.

If something disturbs them, or if the den is not comfortable, they will move about to get more comfortable. They do not need food or water until spring because they survive on the layers of fat stored in their bodies.

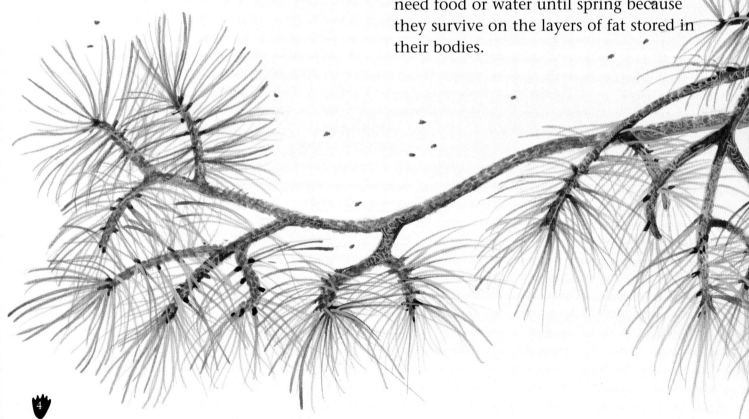

4

Buffalo

The largest prairie mammal
Is called the buffalo;
Vast herds roamed our prairies,
Not very long ago.

But humans came to hunt them,
By the millions they were slain;
We protect them now in buffalo parks,
So the herds grow strong again.

Hundred of years ago, vast herds of buffalo roamed the prairies. Today, only several thousand of these wooly beasts are alive and protected in some national parks. The largest herd in the world is in Wood Buffalo National Park, Alberta, Canada.

When the buffalo were killed off by man, the grizzlies and wolves that depended on the buffalo for food also disappeared.

Buffalo roam in herds that are usually led by an older cow. She is the boss and the watchdog for the herd. She signals when there is danger and is the leader of the search for new places to find grass.

Buffalo are herbivorous. This means they eat various types of grass, vines and lichens. In the winter some of the herds move south, while others stay and find food by clearing away the snow with their strong front hooves and massive heads.

Buffalo have thick curly hair on their foreheads and beards under their chins.

Both the female and male have horns that curve upward. These are true horns that are never shed.

A buffalo cow gives birth to a single calf in the spring and nurses it in the same way as farm cows do. The calf reaches maturity when is around three years old. The buffalo lives to about twenty-five years of age. It is the largest land mammal in North America.

Coyote

The coyote is a wild dog;
Hills and prairies are its home,
It's like a wolf, except that
It likes to hunt alone.

Since they are dogs, coyotes
In daytime like to growl;
But when the moon is shining,
They really like to howl.

Coyotes are sometimes called bush wolves by native Americans. Coyote are bigger than a fox, but smaller than a wolf. They live on the North American prairies in open woodlands or in bushy, rocky areas. Though they are seldom seen, many coyotes now live in cities and towns.

Coyotes will eat almost anything, but they are most fond of rabbits, squirrels, mice, eggs and insects. They also eat dead animals left by other predators.

In the evening they make high-pitched yelping sounds, then a long howl that ends in short, sharp yips. These sounds can be especially scary to campers sleeping in a tent under the stars.

Coyotes are highly intelligent and have been seen cooperating with badgers in digging up ground squirrels.

Some coyotes mate for life. Each spring five to seven pups are born in a den usually dug by the female. A male coyote is a very good father. He does all the hunting for his family from the time the cubs are born until they have learned to hunt for themselves. The pups are about nine months old before they are completely on their own.

Coyotes can run up to fifty kilometers (thirty miles) per hour. They run with their tails downward, while wolves run with their tails pointed upward.

The coyote's enemies include wolves, cougars and man.

Coyotes are extremely cautious animals and appear to look both ways before crossing a highway. Their ability to adapt to new habitats allows them to survive even after catastrophic damage like an earthquake.

The coyote is a very important animal in native legends, in which it is known as the Trickster.

Deer

Most deer live in forests
Since they're secretive and shy;
But some are found in city parks
Where people live nearby.

The big ones are the buck and doe,
The baby is the fawn;
If a deer senses danger,
Suddenly it's gone!

Spotted, wobbly-legged baby deer, called fawns, are born in late spring. Often the mother, called a doe, has twins, and these newborn get to their feet within minutes. During the first two weeks the doe leaves them in a safe hiding spot, but returns often to feed them.

The fawns have very little smell. This, combined with a spotted coat, which acts as a camouflage, helps to protect them from their enemies. When their legs grow stronger they follow their mother and begin nibbling plants, twigs, shrubs, fungi, acorns, grass and herbs.

Deer live in small herds in forests across the southern parts of Canada and all of the United States. They move very gracefully, always looking out for danger. Their enemies are coyotes, wolves, bears, cougars and man.

The winter coat of a deer is like thousands of hollow straws lined up. These hollow hairs trap warm air close to the body and help keep the animal warm. The deer sheds this winter coat in the spring.

Deer live up to twenty years in the wild.

Fox

In many stories foxes
Are said to be quite sly,
But really foxes are just smart
And very, very shy

Foxes like to hunt at night,
Then den up in the day;
Their fur is red or brown or white
Or sometimes silver gray.

The mother fox is called a vixen. After her
three to five pups are born she protects
them by staying safely hidden in her
den.The den can be a spot in the hollow
of a tree, a space between rocks or even a
hole in the ground.

When the pups are about one month old they are big enough to leave the den, and then the fun begins! Outside, they sniff, jump, play with twigs or rocks and chase butterflies and feathers. This play helps them become good hunters.

The father also helps to care for the pups. He carries birds, squirrels and other food back to the family. As the pups get stronger, both parents teach them to pounce on mice, rabbits and frogs, and to search for eggs, insects and fruit.

When fall arrives, the mother forces the pups out of the den, for they must now leave to find a mate and raise families of their own. Foxes do not den near coyotes.

Foxes are about the size of a small dog and move about with an almost catlike grace. Their enemies are man, coyotes, wolves and cougars. They live about six years in the wild.

Mountain Goat

Mountain goats are walkers,
They don't much like to run;
What they really like is climbing
Up a mountain in the sun.

Mountain goats in winter,
Have coats of snowy white;
In summer when they're shedding,
They're a most repulsive sight.

Mountain goats live in the mountains of western Canada and the western United States. They spend most of the year moving about in small herds of about twelve to twenty-five individuals.

In the summertime they graze in the meadows above the timberline. To find food in the winter they must come down to lower levels. There, they find grasses and plants wherever the wind sweeps the mountain faces bare of snow.

Mountain goats' enemies include bears, cougars, wolves and coyotes. They can defend themselves against these predators by moving easily across steep mountain slopes where the predators cannot follow.

In the spring the mother usually has one baby, called a kid, although sometimes she has twins. She looks after them for about a year.

Both the female and male goats have sharp, slightly curved black horns. You can tell the age of a mountain goat by counting the rings—one ring for each year.

Groundhog

On February second,
The groundhog wakes from sleep,
Then leaves its den and steps outside
To give the sky a peep.

If the sky is cloudy,
No shadows on the ground,
It thinks, "Ah, winter's over,
I think I'll stick around."

But if the sky is sunny,
And cold and blue and deep,
It dives back in its burrow,
For six more weeks of sleep.

On February second the groundhog, according to legend, is supposed to wake from his long winter sleep to take a look at the weather. Some people believe that if the groundhog sees its shadow, they will have six more weeks of winter. If it doesn't, spring has finally arrived.

Groundhogs are like small digging machines and can bury themselves out of sight as quick as a wink! These fat furry creatures are members of the squirrel family.

They live in the eastern United States and the woodlands all across Canada.

During the winter they hibernate for several months in their warm cozy burrows under the ground. Sometimes they get restless and stir about. They usually end their long sleep in early March. Then, when it's warm, they come out and start nibbling and eating grass, berries, clover, plants and sometimes corn.

Even though groundhogs prefer having all their feet on the ground, they can climb trees to find food or to get away from enemies.

Should one of their enemies—such as a fox, lynx or coyote—come snooping around, groundhogs signal danger by making shrill calls to warn others.

Female groundhogs usually deliver four to six young in late spring. They nurse their babies for about six weeks.

Lynx

A lynx looks like your cat,
Though it has much bigger feet;
Rabbits, hares and field mice
Are what it likes to eat.

It kind of makes you wonder
What nature had in mind,
When she gave the lynx such different ears
And a short tail out behind.

The lynx hunts rabbits at night in the deep
forests in parts of the United States, Canada
and Mexico. It does not live on the prairies.
Its den is in the hollow of a tree, among
rocks or in bushes.

Its favorite food is the snowshoe hare, but if
it is not quick enough to catch one, it will
settle for rodents, squirrels, birds, a tasty fox
and sometimes even a deer.

The lynx cannot run fast, so it hunts by leaping or pouncing upon its prey. It hunts by sight and sound, not by smell.

In winter the lynx grows heavy fur on the top and bottom of its big feet. These furry feet act like snowshoes to keep it from sinking into the deep soft snow when it is hunting.

On its ears it has stiff black tufts of hair that act like antenna to aid hearing. Its excellent eyesight allows the lynx to spot a mouse at seventy-five meters (240 feet) and a hare at one kilometer (about half a mile).

Every two years the mother lynx has a litter of four to six kittens, which she looks after all by herself. Usually, a mother lynx must kill every other night to feed herself and her kittens.

Lynx populations rise and fall in response to snowshoe hare populations. Because the lynx is a predator and an excellent fighter, it has no enemies other than man. Other predators such as a cougars and wolves could not afford to be wounded by this wildcat.

The lynx is the most common wildcat in Canada.

Moose

A moose's body is thick and wide,
With stiltlike legs below;
These help a moose in wintertime
To wander through deep snow.

A mother moose gives birth to twins
In June or late in May;
And when these calves are one year old,
She sends them on their way.

Moose live in the forests and marshlands across the southern part of Canada and the northern part of the United States. Males, called bulls, usually live by themselves, joining the females only at mating time. The females, called cows, usually stay with the calves born for a year.

Calves are helpless at birth, so the mother moose, hides them in the bush away from their enemies: bears, wolves, wildcats, wolverines and man. The voice of a newborn calf is a low grunt, but after a few days it develops a wail that sounds just like a human baby.

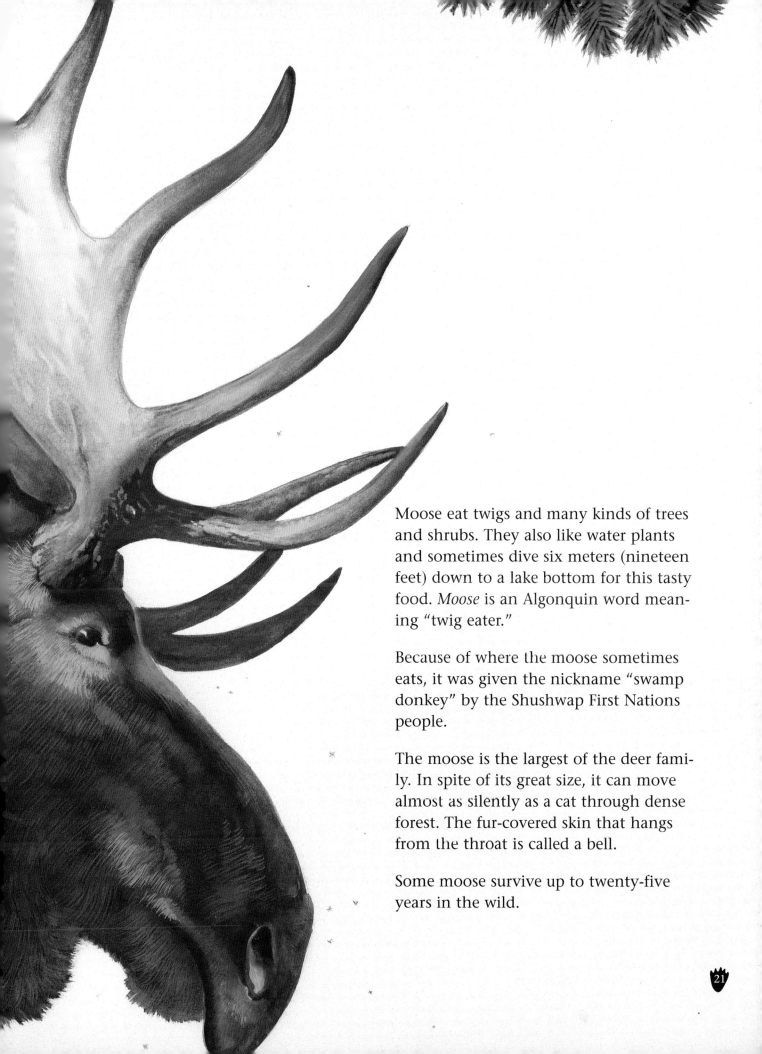

Moose eat twigs and many kinds of trees and shrubs. They also like water plants and sometimes dive six meters (nineteen feet) down to a lake bottom for this tasty food. *Moose* is an Algonquin word meaning "twig eater."

Because of where the moose sometimes eats, it was given the nickname "swamp donkey" by the Shushwap First Nations people.

The moose is the largest of the deer family. In spite of its great size, it can move almost as silently as a cat through dense forest. The fur-covered skin that hangs from the throat is called a bell.

Some moose survive up to twenty-five years in the wild.

River Otter

An otter feels at home on land,
But much prefers the water;
When splashing in a river,
It's doing what it "otter."

Otters like to be amused,
They really like to play;
Sliding down a muddy bank
Is fun for them each day.

It's fun to watch otters at play. They will slide and tumble down the steep banks of streams or lakes into the water, looking just like children tobogganing down a snowy slope.

River otters live near rivers and large lakes all across Canada and the northern parts of the United States.

Otters dig their dens along the riverbanks with the entrances below the water. This way they can dive into the water, slip into their dens and escape from their enemies, which are cougars, wolverine, wolves and man.

Otters are swift and skillful swimmers. They can easily catch the fish, frogs, crayfish and other water animals that are their food.

When the otters dive, their ears close so no water can enter. Their eyes are excellent for seeing underwater. Their glossy brown fur is thick and waterproof. At one time it was used for fur coats.

A mother otter gives birth to one to five babies in the spring. The young otters stay with their mother for nearly a year. She teaches them to swim and fish and to lie quietly or dive when danger is near.

Otters have a basic instinct to return to their original home. One true story tells of how two otters held in Vancouver returned home over the Georgia Strait and found their way back to Victoria sixty-six kilometers (forty miles) away.

Porcupine

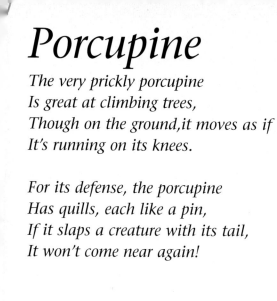

The very prickly porcupine
Is great at climbing trees,
Though on the ground, it moves as if
It's running on its knees.

For its defense, the porcupine
Has quills, each like a pin,
If it slaps a creature with its tail,
It won't come near again!

The porcupine can afford to be brave. It wears a suit of thirty thousand sharp, barbed quills. When an enemy comes too close, the porcupine turns its back and lashes its tail to one side. The quills will then stick into any nearby paw, face or foot. An experienced hunter such as the wolf will roll the porcupine on its back to avoid its quills before killing it.

The porcupine lives in the forests and open country across Canada, the United States and northern Mexico. It moves clumsily through the forest, usually at night.

During the day it can often be seen hunched into a large black ball in a tree. Its home is a nest in a log, cave or hollow tree.

The porcupine eats bark, buds, berries and the leaves of trees. It also likes salt, and many get killed trying to lick the salt used to melt snow on winter highways.

The female porcupine gives birth to only one baby each spring. It is born with its eyes open and can climb a tree almost immediately. Its quills are soft at birth, but they harden after one hour, ready to be used for defense. The baby stays with the mother for about a month.

Rabbit

The soft and furry rabbit
Likes to feed at night,
Avoiding hungry owls
By keeping out of sight!

This long-legged rabbit
Can speed off in high gear;
And many, many rabbits
Join the family every year.

A rabbit must be very careful not to become a dinner for one of its many enemies: the fox, lynx, weasel, owl and coyote.

Its brownish summer fur turns white in winter, but its fluffy tail is always white and looks like a powder puff. Could you imagine if your hair changed color to white in winter, then back to its normal color in summer?

Soft, furry rabbits live in the woodlands and prairies all across Canada and the northern parts of the United States.

During the day rabbits stay safely in their lairs or burrows. At night they come out to feed on grasses and other plants. Rabbits are total vegetarians. In the winter they tunnel in the snow to keep warm and find food.

A mother rabbit can give birth to as many as twenty-five babies each year. She makes a nest by plucking fur from around her chest and abdomen. This fur keeps the newborns warm and cosy. The young nurse only two times a day, and are on their own in about a month.

When frightened, rabbits thump the ground with a back leg to warn nearby rabbits. The doe, or female rabbit, is larger than the male rabbit, which is called a buck.

Raccoon

Raccoons look like burglars,
With that mask across their face;
All day they sleep, but in the night
They steal from place to place.

Perhaps you own a panda bear,
A stuffed one, and quite tame;
You can tell these two are cousins—
Their faces look the same.

Most raccoons live in the forests across United States and southern Canada, but some live in cities. The city raccoons look for food in garbage cans or in people's gardens. Raccoons have adapted to city living better than most wild animals.

Raccoons use their hands, and they are excellent climbers. They have an interesting habit of playing with their food in water before eating it. If there is no water they still rub the food with their hands.

Nighttime is when raccoons usually search for their meals. They eat crayfish, bird's eggs, fruit, nuts, acorns and the seeds of many plants. Riverbanks are a favorite hunting place.

A raccoon's home is usually a den in the hollow of a tree or in a log or a burrow in the ground.

The female raccoon has two to five young each year. Babies are born in the spring and stay with their mothers throughout the first winter. They live for about sixteen years in the wild and about twenty years in captivity.

Adult raccoons have few enemies other than man, but baby raccoons are sometimes attacked by owls, foxes, coyotes, wolves and dogs.

Raccoons are found in all provinces of Canada except Newfoundland, and in all parts of the United States.

Skunk

The creatures we call skunks
Are famous for their smell;
And all across this country
These little stinkers dwell.

They are black and white and furry,
Just as cuddly as can be,
But if by chance you get too close,
PHEW-EE!

A skunk may look pretty, but stay away!
It has musk glands, and when frightened,
it sprays out a strong horrible stink. Many
an unwary person, dog or cat has had to
bathe in tomato juice to get rid of the
smell after being squirted by a skunk.

The skunk's black and white markings
and smelly spray protect it against its
enemies. The exceptions are predatory
birds such as owls, eagles and hawks that
have little sense of smell and will attack
a skunk. Its chief enemy is the great
horned owl.

Skunks are night creatures, hunting and scavenging when it is dark and sleeping during the day. Skunks eat mice, eggs, insects, grubs, berries and dead, rotting animal flesh.

They make their dens in burrows, under boulders, in wood piles or in deserted buildings. Female skunks will often live together in the same area and even share their dens.

Six to eight kittens are born to the mother skunk. Babies are blind at birth and do not see for about eighteen days. At first they nurse and eat what the mother brings them, but quickly they are able to hunt for themselves.

Skunks live in woodlands and grasslands from Canada to northern Mexico. A skunk is about the size of a large domestic cat.

Published by
Grasshopper Books Publishing
106 Waddington Drive
Kamloops, British Columbia
Canada V2E 1M2

This book is dedicated to my favorite youngest daughter Heather-Faye Mastin and to Bob Gunson.

Acknowledgements:
The author wishes to thank the following for their help and contributions to this book: the governments of Canada and British Columbia, Josh Lockwood, Dawn Brodie, Bill Gilroy of the Kamloops Wildlife Park, and her family.

Canadian Cataloguing in Publication Data
Mastin, Colleayn O. (Colleayn Olive)
North American wild animals

(Grasshopper series; 1)
Includes index.
ISBN 1-895910-21-8

1. Zoology—North American—Juvenile literature. 2 Zoology— North American—Poetry. I. Sovak, Jan, 1953– II. Title. III. Series: Mastin, Colleayn O. (Colleayn Olive), Grasshopper Series; 1.
QL715.M255 1997   j591.97   C97-910364-9

Printed in Canada